DATE DUE		
SEP 2 2012		
OCT 2 2012		
4/14/16		

The Urbana Free Library

To renew: call 217-367-4057
or go to "*urbanafreelibrary.org*"
and select "Renew/Request Items"

CHILDREN'S ILLUSTRATORS

MO WILLEMS

Sheila Griffin Llanas

ABDO Publishing Company

visit us at
www.abdopublishing.com

7-12
25⁰⁰

Published by ABDO Publishing Company, PO Box 398166, Minneapolis, MN 55439. Copyright © 2012 by Abdo Consulting Group, Inc. International copyrights reserved in all countries. No part of this book may be reproduced in any form without written permission from the publisher. The Checkerboard Library™ is a trademark and logo of ABDO Publishing Company.

Printed in the United States of America, North Mankato, Minnesota.
102011
012012

 PRINTED ON RECYCLED PAPER

Cover Photo: Marty Umans / Disney•Hyperion
Interior Photos: Alamy p. 21; courtesy Mo Willems pp. 5, 6, 7, 9, 10, 11, 13, 17
    From Mo Willems' *Don't Let the Pigeon Drive the Bus* Copyright © 2003 by Mo Willems. Reprinted by Permission of Disney•Hyperion, an imprint of Disney Book Group LLC. All rights reserved. p. 14
    From Mo Willems' *Knuffle Bunny: A Cautionary Tale* Copyright © 2004 by Mo Willems. Reprinted by Permission of Disney•Hyperion, an imprint of Disney Book Group LLC. All rights reserved. p. 16
    From Mo Willems' *Naked Mole Rat Gets Dressed* Copyright © 2008 by Mo Willems. Reprinted by Permission of Disney•Hyperion, an imprint of Disney Book Group LLC. All rights reserved. p. 19
    From Mo Willems' *There is a Bird on Your Head* Copyright © 2007 by Mo Willems. Reprinted by Permission of Disney•Hyperion, an imprint of Disney Book Group LLC. All rights reserved. p. 19

Series Coordinator: BreAnn Rumsch / Editors: Megan M. Gunderson, BreAnn Rumsch
Art Direction: Neil Klinepier

Library of Congress Cataloging-in-Publication Data

Llanas, Sheila Griffin, 1958-
 Mo Willems / Sheila Griffin Llanas.
     p. cm. -- (Children's illustrators)
 Includes index.
 ISBN 978-1-61783-249-9
 1. Willems, Mo--Juvenile literature. 2. Illustrators--United States--Biography--Juvenile literature. I. Willems, Mo. II. Title.
 NC975.5.W519L59 2012
 741.6'42--dc23
                                2011030112

CONTENTS

The Importance of Doodling

Award-winning author and illustrator Mo Willems has not always made picture books. As a young man, he wrote cartoon strips and practiced stand-up comedy. He later made **animated** films and wrote television cartoons. Today, Willems's long history with humor helps him entertain young readers everywhere.

Another talent has helped Willems find success, too. Some of his best books began with simple doodles! Needless to say, doodling is extremely important to Willems. So at his home, the dining room walls are painted like a dark green chalkboard. Butcher paper often covers the table. There, friends and family have "group draws."

When Willems visits schools and libraries, he likes to have fun with his audiences. He also cares about inspiring his fans. He often asks children if they like to make up stories or draw. Then he says that makes them authors and illustrators, just like he is.

Willems's house is lovingly known as "Knuffle Manor."

YOUNG MO

Mo Willems was born in Chicago, Illinois, on February 11, 1968. This was just a few months after his parents, Casey and Constance, had emigrated from Holland. The family soon moved to New Orleans, Louisiana. There, Mo's father worked in hotel management and his mother studied law.

Growing up, Mo spent hours looking at drawings by Dutch artist Fiep Westendorp. Though he did not own many American children's books, he loved Charles Schulz's comic strip *Peanuts*. As a lonely kid, he could especially relate to the character Charlie Brown.

Young Mo loved to sketch Snoopy and Charlie Brown. He dreamed of becoming a cartoonist. Mo even wrote a letter to Schulz. "Dear Mr. Schulz,"

Baby Mo

it said. "Can I have your job when you're dead?" But he never received a reply. Mo's father never mailed that letter!

As a kid, Mo was always drawing!

When Mo started third grade, his mother became a lawyer. Then, Mo's father quit his hotel job. Casey became a potter and opened his own **ceramics** studio.

Mo liked to visit the studio. There, his father taught him how to make pots and work with ceramics. Casey's pottery was not just artwork. It was meant to be useful. One of his designs was a berry bowl. Holes in the bottom let water drain out. Mo liked that his father's creations were for more than just looking at.

COMEDY AND CARTOONS

By high school, Mo had developed a zany sense of humor. He even performed stand-up comedy. Mo also acted in school plays. And, he liked visiting art museums. He thought the museums were like "spaceships filled with ideas made physical." He especially liked the **abstract** art of Pablo Picasso, Paul Klee, and Alexander Calder.

As he grew up, Mo remained a fan of comics. He added *Spider-Man*, *Doonesbury*, and *Calvin and Hobbes* to his list of favorites. Mo also started drawing his own comic strips. One appeared in his school newspaper. And eventually, one was published every week in a **real estate** magazine! The strip was called *Surrealty*.

After graduating in 1986, Mo traveled to London, England. There, he practiced performing his stand-up comedy. This helped him develop better timing for his jokes. It also helped him learn which jokes worked and which ones did not.

That fall, Mo started college at New York University's Tisch School of the Arts. At first he studied filmmaking, but he soon switched his focus to **animation**. In his free time, Mo performed with a comedy group called the Sterile Yak.

In his heart, Willems has always thought of himself as a cartoonist.

SUNNY DAYS

Willems finished college in 1990 and graduated with **honors**. He wanted to be a comedian. But he wasn't sure

where his goals would lead him. So he soon set out on a trip around the world. During his year of traveling, he backpacked in 30 countries. Each day, he drew a cartoon.

In 1993, Willems moved to Brooklyn, New York. There, he found work making short films. The next year, Willems got an important break. He was hired to write for *Sesame Street*.

Willems likes to keep his books simple, yet funny. This approach comes from the lessons he learned working in television.

Willems already knew how to write comedy for adults. But in this new job, he learned to write comedy for children. He wrote funny **scripts** and even created the character

Willems enjoyed working on Sesame Street. He felt the show was simple, magical, and kooky.

Suzie Kabloozie. Willems was happy to learn how much he enjoyed writing for children.

In 1995, Nickelodeon hired Willems to create a new **animated** cartoon. It was called *The Off-Beats*. Though Willems **excelled** at animation, it was hard work. One cartoon could take 22,000 drawings, hundreds of people, and 16 months to make!

BUILDING A CAREER

Willems worked on *The Off-Beats* for three years. During that time, he met and fell in love with a woman named Cheryl Camp. She worked in television too, making commercials. They married in 1997 and remained in Brooklyn. The couple later welcomed a daughter named Trixie.

After marrying, Willems felt ready to try something new with his career. So, he took time off of work and traveled back to Europe. Willems spent about a month in Oxford, England, where he tried to write great children's books. He later admitted they were terrible!

Back in the United States, Willems returned to his television work. He was still writing for *Sesame Street*. During his nine seasons with the show, he earned six **Emmy Awards**. Then in 2000, he created *Sheep in the Big City* for Cartoon Network.

Mo and Cheryl

Things were going well. Then one day, Willems learned a lesson from a young fan. "It looks like you're trying too hard," the viewer wrote. Willems was surprised. Wasn't trying hard a good thing? He knew that making television shows was **complicated**. But, he realized that entertainment should still seem effortless!

PUBLISHING THE PIGEON

Willems kept busy with his work, but he began to explore a new artistic vision. In 2002, he wrote for the Cartoon Network show *Codename: Kids Next Door*. In his spare time, he continued writing and doodling. Every year, he collected his doodles in a sketchbook. He would give copies of it to family and friends as gifts.

While in England, Willems had started drawing a funny pigeon. Eventually, the Pigeon made it into one of his sketchbooks. Willems never thought his

The Pigeon appears in every Willems book. Willems claims the Pigeon sneaks himself in!

doodles would be published. Still, he showed them to his agent. When she saw his pigeon sketchbook, she said, "I think there's a book in that!"

Eventually, Willems's agent called with exciting news. The Pigeon would appear in his own book! *Don't Let the Pigeon Drive the Bus!* was published in 2003.

Willems wondered if a single person would read his first picture book. He should not have worried because readers loved it! It even became a *New York Times* best seller.

That first pigeon book changed Willems's life. He finally left television to focus on books. And in 2004, the story was named a **Caldecott Honor Book**. That same year, Willems published *The Pigeon Finds a Hotdog!* It looked like the Pigeon was here to stay, and Willems had found a new passion.

ELEMENTS OF ART: SHAPE

Shape is one of the basic parts of art. Shapes are formed when lines come together. They can be geometric, such as circles, squares, and triangles. Or, they can be irregular and squiggly. These types of shapes are considered organic.

Artists often begin sketches with just basic shapes. Willems creates his characters from simple shapes. He does this on purpose so that young children can recreate his funny characters, such as the Pigeon.

KNUFFLE BUNNY

Willems got the idea for his next book from his own family. The story is about a father trying to find his daughter's favorite stuffed toy. He based the toy on a Dutch word his parents used, *knuffel*. It means to hug or snuggle.

At first, Willems wasn't sure what animal to choose for the stuffed toy. He tried a knuffle bear, but he could not make the bear show emotion. Next, he tried a knuffle bunny. It worked! Willems found that if he drew its ears up, down, or sideways, the bunny looked happy, sad, or afraid.

KNUFFLE BUNNY

A CAUTIONARY TALE BY Mo Willems
WINNER OF A CALDECOTT HONOR FOR DON'T LET THE PIGEON DRIVE THE BUS!

Willems likes to say that "everything in that book is true except the parts I made up."

For the book's artwork, Willems tried a new **technique**. He took photographs of his New York neighborhood. These became the backgrounds for his ink drawings. *Knuffle Bunny: A Cautionary Tale* was published in 2004.

Knuffle Bunny proved to be another big hit. It was named a 2005 **Caldecott Honor Book**. Its **sequel**, *Knuffle Bunny Too: A Case of Mistaken Identity*, followed in 2007. It earned a 2008 Caldecott Honor.

Willems is often inspired by his daughter, Trixie. He named the little girl in the Knuffle Bunny books after her.

CREATIVE VISION

Willems had been living in New York for more than 20 years. In 2008, he decided it was time for a change. So, the family moved to quiet, peaceful Northampton, Massachusetts.

Meanwhile, Willems had been developing his popular Elephant and Piggie series. *There Is a Bird on Your Head* earned a **Theodor Seuss Geisel Medal** in 2008. He won a Geisel Medal again the next year for *Are You Ready to Play Outside?* And in 2011, he earned a Geisel Honor for *We Are in a Book!*

Willems creates new stories in his art studio on the top floor of his house. **Mobiles** and stuffed toys decorate the space. His published books line his shelves. And, color-coded charts track his progress on new projects.

Willems starts a new book with an idea that makes him laugh. Then he doodles a lot, creating various situations. Finally, he plays around with paper, pencils, and colors. He also decides the size and shape of the pages.

Naked Mole Rat Gets Dressed

Mo Willems

So far, Willems has created 6 Pigeon books, 3 Knuffle Bunny books, and 16 Elephant and Piggie books! He also created a series called Cat the Cat. Other popular books include *Leonardo the Terrible Monster, Hooray for Amanda and Her Alligator!*, and *Naked Mole Rat Gets Dressed*.

An **ELEPHANT & PIGGIE** Book

There Is a Bird on Your Head!

By **Mo Willems**

Playful Books

Success has continued to follow Willems. In 2010, he published *Knuffle Bunny Free: An Unexpected Diversion*. This story was the third in the Knuffle Bunny **trilogy**.

But Knuffle Bunny wasn't finished yet! That same year, Willems wrote *Knuffle Bunny: A Cautionary Musical*. It was based on the first book. Meanwhile, Willems and his wife and daughter also recorded **audio** versions of the Knuffle Bunny books.

Though Willems is busy making books, he still finds time to write a blog called *Mo Willems Doodles*. Writing as the Pigeon, he also posts funny updates on Twitter. In his free time, Willems especially likes to be at home. There, he can hang out with Trixie, work in his garden, and build sculptures made of metal and wire.

Willems loves to say that his books are not only for reading but for playing. Just like his father's pottery, Willems wants his creations to be useful. He hopes readers will draw the characters, write new scenes, and act out skits. So, he pours his many creative skills into each of his picture books. No wonder fans are excited to see what Willems will come up with next!

Willems hopes his stories inspire young readers to make their own stories and art.

GLOSSARY

abstract - in art, expressing ideas or emotions without attempting to create a realistic picture.

animated - made using a process that involves a projected series of drawings. They appear to move due to slight changes in each drawing. Animation is the process of making something animated.

audio - of or relating to the sound that is heard on a recording or broadcast.

Caldecott Honor Book - a runner-up for the Caldecott Medal. The Caldecott Medal is an award the American Library Association gives to the artist who illustrated the year's best picture book.

ceramic - of or relating to a product such as porcelain or brick. It is made from heating a mineral, such as clay, at high temperatures.

complicated - hard to understand, explain, or deal with.

Emmy Award - one of several awards the Academy of Television Arts and Sciences presents to the year's best television programs, writers, and actors.

excel - to be better than others.

honors - special attention given to a graduating student for high academic achievement.

mobile (MOH-beel) - a decoration or work of art that is hung from above. It has attached shapes or figures that move easily in the air.

real estate - property, including buildings and land. It is also the business of selling such property.

script - the written words and directions used to put on a play or a movie.

sequel - a book, movie, or other work that continues the story begun in a preceding one.

technique - a method or style in which something is done.

Theodore Seuss Geisel Medal - an award given to the author and illustrator of the best English-language book for beginning readers published during the preceding year. A runner-up receives a Theodore Seuss Geisel Honor.

trilogy - a series of three novels, movies, or other works that are closely related and involve the same characters or themes.

WEB SITES

To learn more about Mo Willems, visit ABDO Publishing Company online. Web sites about Mo Willems are featured on our Book Links page. These links are routinely monitored and updated to provide the most current information available.
www.abdopublishing.com

INDEX